# Ugly Church

Andrew D. Marshall

*uglychurch.org*

Connect with Ugly Church
on Facebook
and Instagram

All quotations are from The Holy Bible: New International Version. Copyright 1973, 1978, 1984, 2011. Biblia, Inc.

Captain America reference from:

Captain America: The First Avenger. Directed by Joe Johnston.

Performance by Chris Evans. Marvel Entertainment, 2011.

# Ugly Church

Andrew D. Marshall

*uglychurch.org*

Connect with Ugly Church

on Facebook

and Instagram

# Contents

# Introduction

It all started with a few conversations about struggling churches and struggling communities. One had lost touch and the other had lost hope. Increasingly, it seemed that the only churches that weren't struggling were the ones not in struggling neighborhoods. Church plants popped up in the more comfortable suburbs and exurbs, targeting the middle and upper-middle classes. Resources funneled into attractive buildings and high-tech programs. Struggling churches and communities continued to struggle. The needle, on that score, didn't seem to flinch. So, it became a topic of conversation that turned into a point of conviction: the Church needs to change.

First, I think we need to be clear on what the Church is. The Church is the body of Christ, the physical presence of Christ on earth. It's comprised of believers called out of the world, transformed by grace, and thrust back into the world to work and witness for Christ and the Kingdom. Even though the Church is often confused with its property and programs, it's the people of God that makes the Church.

I love the Church. I love the mish-mash diversity of its members, the redemptive promise of broken people being restored and recreated into something new and beautiful. I love that the Church is God's chosen instrument through which to engage the world, even with her warts and wrinkles. Sometimes I think it's ridiculous that God would choose to use something as ungainly and awkward as the Church to represent Him and His mission.

I've had the privilege of experiencing varied expressions of the Church from rural Appalachia to urban Portland, Oregon, small town Washington State to metro Boston. My observations, obviously, are my own; I don't pretend to know every situation in every context. The stories shared are primarily from personal experience or from first-hand accounts. My hope is that through these stories and snapshots a conversation will be sparked about the disconnect between the Church and those most desperately in need of Christ and that out of those conversations, changes will come.

## My Story

I grew up in rural Tennessee, in the foothills of the Appalachians, in the late 70s and early 80s. My dad pastored a small country church accessible only by a dirt road that twice forded a creek. For my father's service, he was granted a small parsonage in much need of repair and an even smaller stipend. We lived by the work of our hands on the two or so acres attached to the parsonage, growing vegetables and raising pigs, cows, and chickens. We were poor but not impoverished. More significantly, we were well-off by the living standards of many around us, the hole in the bathroom floor notwithstanding.

Those years formed much of my understanding of what it means to be "working poor." Our neighbors toiled in tobacco fields and various trades, never scratching out much more than a basic living. Some didn't even manage that. Even so, I've never lived anywhere that exemplified generosity and gratitude more completely.

My adolescence would find my family on the edge of a larger town in Tennessee, a wealthy Oregon suburb, and then a logging town in the Cascade Mountains. A failed first attempt at Bible college would take me to Seattle, where I would later be homeless and living in a '72 Plymouth. After a few years of chasing rock star dreams, marriage, and settling into a job and homeownership, a second stab at Bible college would lead to Portland and learning to minister to troubled youth, previously incarcerated, and sufferers of addiction. After a stop-over in the Columbia Gorge to help plant a church, the last 8 years have been spent pastoring in the Boston metro area, attempting to affect the change proposed in this writing.

In 2016, the church sold a million-dollar-plus property in the comfortable suburbs on the north side of our city to intentionally relocate to the highly diverse and working-class south side. The church's 90-year history saw it flee the south side where it began, incrementally moving from the diversifying downtown into the whiter and wealthier suburbs. By moving back into the city's core, we're declaring our solidarity with our most disadvantaged neighbors. As a church, we're learning to get "ugly" and that ugly is a good thing.

As you read this, my prayer is that you will think ugly is a good thing, too, and turn your church into the "ugly" thing Christ intended.

# Chapter

# 1

# Why We Need to Get Ugly

The Church has gotten too pretty, and I'm not talking about the architecture. If you search Google Images for "ugly church," you will be rewarded with some of the most bizarre, outlandish, and unattractive structures built for the purpose of housing a congregation. Many are more akin to spaceships or microorganisms than buildings. They aren't instantly recognizable as a "church." But far more worrisome than some of the Church's buildings is that often the Church herself isn't instantly recognizable as the body of Christ. It's just too pretty.

What do I mean by pretty? The Church in America is clean, dressed up, smells good, and constantly smiling. It's like that person you admire but don't want to stand next to lest your inadequacies start showing. It's like the restaurant you would like to try out but you're not sure you can afford it or have the right clothes to wear. It's like the doctor's office you avoid because you're waiting to lose those thirty pounds you know the doctor will be pointing out. It's like a secret club where you have to know the password to get in.

A "pretty" church seeks to attract "pretty" people. The pretty church is one where everyone is "fine" even if they aren't. It's where your best face is put forward, a false front to mask the realities of your life. It's the kind of place where you feel like you need to be somehow better than you are.

It's also the kind of place, unfortunately, where you wonder if you even belong. You worry that you'll drag some part of real life in on your shoe and someone will point you to the exit. It's also a place that makes you wonder if you're the only one with problems, fears, doubts, and disappointments. And you may ask yourself, should I bring my traveling circus of struggles and insecurities into a place where everyone seems to have it all together? Frankly, you may feel too ugly to fit in.

So, what about the "ugly" people? Ugly, in this instance, has nothing to do with appearance. "Ugly" refers to the situations and circumstances surrounding a person that causes them to be "repulsive" or to keep others--even Christians--away. Things like addiction, homelessness, chronic illness, poverty, abuse, domestic dysfunction, mental illness, incarceration, fatherlessness, abandonment, loneliness, and countless other elements that repel rather than attract. Where are the churches for the outsiders and the outcasts? For the least, the last, and the lost? I'm not suggesting there aren't ugly churches in existence doing great things for the Kingdom of God, but I do believe there are far too few of them. Certainly there are too few of them in a world filled with people who would consider themselves "ugly" if you had an honest conversation with them.

# Defining an Ugly Church

An ugly church can meet in a cathedral, a multi-million dollar facility, a '60s era church building resembling an upside-down ark, a storefront, or under a highway overpass. It is not defined by where it meets, nor the size of its building or bank account. They can be found in the grittiest urban core, the remotest Native American village, the wealthiest beach-side community and the most common suburb. It is not defined by its appearance or its location. It is defined by its adherence to the mission and message of Christ. It is defined by closely following the steps of its scandalous Savior. Simply put, the Church should be found where one would expect to find Jesus if He were walking the earth here and now, and filled with the people for whom His heart broke.

An ugly church is both welcoming to the outsider and the outcast, and also present in the margins and fringes. It's hard for a church to get truly and honestly ugly while keeping a clubhouse mentality. It's the rare church that would overtly shun the smelliest, dirtiest, hopeless "sinner" that darkens the door, but just as rare are those

**It's the rare church that would overtly shun the smelliest, dirtiest, hopeless "sinner" that darkens the door, but just as rare are those seeking them out.** seeking them out. The ugly church is one that is not only sent but goes. As Christ's body, it goes into the world, to the dark and desperate places where we would expect to find Jesus. And it does so, not in condescension and pity, but in humility and compassion. An ugly church is full of people who know where they came from and from what they were saved.

As I look at my own congregation, I ask myself, "Would Jesus come to this church? Would He fit in here, or would He--and His unwieldy and reckless love--feel out of place?" What I'm really asking is, "Are we an active part of His church? Do we love others in the neighborhood and community around us in the same unwieldy and reckless way He loves us?"

The more I look around, the more I see Jesus in places the pretty church is too reluctant to go. I see Jesus driving a young man to the free clinic, praying with a heroin addict on a street corner, and kneeling with an immigrant on a sidewalk. Most often these days, I see Him hanging out on the corner across from a boarded-up convenience store where the addicted, broke, and broken congregate. Occasionally, His

**The more I look around, the more I see Jesus in places the pretty church is too reluctant to go.**

Church shows up to offer a meal or a word of encouragement. Too rarely does it stay to find out about Patty's sister who overdosed (and Patty's own losing battle with alcohol), or listen to Raymond's rambling stories, or how Kyle is dealing with his cystic fibrosis while living on the street. Too few stick around to celebrate Rinaldo's green card and new job, or Jannatil's GED diploma. Too few are willing to engage for the long haul, to befriend and live in relationship with them, to not say a single prayer in passing but to prayerfully and purposefully love them on an ongoing basis.

The ugly church doesn't just engage in "drive by" missions or evangelism. It doesn't swoop into low-income communities with turkeys on Thanksgiving or backpacks at the beginning of a new school year, only to return to its comfortable cloister elsewhere. It doesn't just collect food for the hungry, but intentionally breaks bread with them. The ugly church chooses to "live by" those that others would rather "drive by." My friend, Kurt Gerrold, who can best be described as a "street pastor" sums up the ethic of the ugly church: "to go where no one wants to go, to be with people no one wants to be with." It's especially the "be with" that sets the ugly church apart.

Even though I've been talking about poorer communities, "ugliness" and brokenness exist even in well-heeled neighborhoods. There are families going through divorce, disability, and bankruptcy. There are families with teenagers addicted to pills and pornography. There are families struggling through chronic illness or trying to figure out how to parent a child with special needs. When debts and doubts mount, or it becomes unbearable to lie and respond to every "how are you" with "fine, thanks", is the Church the first place to find solace? Or is it a place to avoid until things get better? Being human is messy business and we're compelled to keep our messiness to ourselves and avoid that of others.  An ugly church, in contrast, wades into the mess with love, humility, and understanding. After all, it's what Jesus would do.

## Jesus' Ugly Ministry

The most compelling argument for Christ's church to "get ugly" is the example He set.  Jesus spent time with the Pharisees and scribes, with the rulers of the synagogue and people of affluence. But even though He ate with those that had no idea they were sick, He preferred to spend His time and energy on those who knew they needed a Healer who could offer them hope. So Jesus spent His time with liars, thieves, and scoundrels.  He freely engaged with men and women of questionable character.  He busied Himself with the sick and the suffering, the wayward and the wounded.  He spent time with the tormented among the tombs and gave the dead new life.

Perhaps the most shocking things Jesus did was to purposeful-ly make physical contact with the lepers and others considered "unclean." In the face of all that was considered to be right and proper, Jesus touched the leper to make him clean. But Jesus wasn't made unclean. Jesus lost nothing in the transaction, but the leper gained everything. This realization heralded a turning point in my understanding of how we--the Church, the physical presence of Christ on earth--are to engage the world. Touching lepers is an ugly business. It's uncomfortable, inconvenient, and (if we're being honest with ourselves) undesirable. If we were to be honest, we'd rather avoid it altogether. Praying for someone's heartbreaking situation should not encompass the entirety of our involvement with the suffering. It's relatively easy to pray (and it makes us feel good); it's another thing altogether to enter into the heartbreak. Just as Jesus could have stood His distance and healed from afar, the need of the leper was more than physical. He needed to be welcomed back into community, to be given value, to be declared worthy of love.

In North America, we deal more with metaphorical leprosy. Many live on the margins and edges of our society, and while they don't have a repulsive skin disease, they have situations, struggles, and circumstances in their lives that repel others. Sadly, many of these things also repel those of us in the Church. Maybe they remind us where we've come from or even of the ugliness inside ourselves we're doing our best to keep hidden. There's a pride, I think, in the Church that makes us forget that we didn't earn our salvation or get cleaned up (sanctified, if you prefer) on our own. Even though we've been saved by grace through faith (read Ephesians 2:1-10), we falsely think that we had to work for our righteousness, so we do what we need to do to preserve it. If that means pursuing holiness by avoidance (purity) and eschewing holiness by engagement (justice), so be it, we say. Let them get themselves sorted out and cleaned up, then they can come join us. But that isn't the way of Jesus. And this is why the Church so often looks so little like Jesus.

Again and again I find myself returning to Jesus's parable of the Pharisee and the tax collector (Luke 18:9-14). In case you're not familiar, the story is of a religious leader full of self-righteousness and a sinner with no illusions. The Pharisee's prayer is a declaration of his own good deeds and superiority over the lowly tax collector.

In contrast, the tax collector's prayer stabs me in the heart every time: "Have mercy on me, a sinner!" With eyes downcast, he beats his chest, and stands at a distance, taking on the posture of the "ugly." My eyes well up every time I think about it, because in my heart I am the tax collector, even as I play the role of Pharisee. Jesus says at the end of the parable, "This man, rather than the other, went home justified before God." It brings me to this question: would the "tax collector" feel welcome in our churches? Together, would we beat our breasts, or simply declare our righteousness to one another?

Jesus's ministry called out the empty, hypocritical religiosity for the sham it is. The call to give up everything (see the rich young ruler), to have nothing (no place to lay His head), or to eat His flesh and drink His blood seemed tailor-made to put people off. Following Jesus is ugly business if it's done right, so He made it clear from the get-go what potential disciples would face. He was clear about the sacrifice, surrender, and service required, the cross each disciple must bear to follow in His footsteps. Somehow, we've spiritualized all the hard stuff away. What's left is pretty, but bland

and unappetizing.

I know I'm not the first to think or say it, but Jesus would be considered too radical for most of our churches. Frankly, He'd make us uncomfortable. He'd be pushing to get folks in the Church onto the streets and into the lives of their neighbors. He'd be constantly challenging us to go deeper in our faith and urging us to turn our belief into behavior. He'd pick apart our budgets and prioritize people over property and programs. He may even kick over some tables in the process...

When I was fresh out of high school and a freshman at a small Bible college, I had a roommate named Nate that made everyone around him uncomfortable. He had the audacity to believe that Jesus meant what He said. (Such as loving God with all you have and all you are, and loving your neighbor like yourself. And expressing love for Christ through obeying the commands Jesus gave. Stuff like that). Nate had the fervor and zeal of a new believer, because he was new. Less than a year before enrolling, he was living in his van and looking constantly for his next high. After meeting Jesus, Nate's life spun 180 degrees and the only thing he wanted was more of Jesus in his life. And he

**The world needs the real Jesus. Not self-help Jesus. Not prosperity Jesus. Not social club Jesus. Not a sanitized, safe, or diluted Jesus. The world needs the radical, audacious, and revolutionary Son of God, full of grace and compassion for the least of us, willing to die for the worst of us, and offering real and abundant life to all of us.**

made the assumption that if we were all at Bible college, we must feel the same way. He would become very disappointed and disillusioned at the tepid response to his enthusiasm. Nate would drop out after two years, not because he fell back into his old life, but because he had a hard time finding Jesus in that place. While many of us were content with a comfortable, watered-down Jesus, Nate wanted the real deal. It makes me wonder: how many people leave the Church because, try as they might, they just can't find Jesus there?

The world needs the real Jesus. Not self-help Jesus. Not prosperity Jesus. Not social club Jesus. Not a sanitized, safe, or diluted Jesus. The world needs the radical, audacious, and revolutionary Son of God, full of grace and compassion for the least of us, willing to die for the worst of us, and offering real and abundant life to all of us.

# Chapter

# 2

# The Leper in Each of Us

Recently, my wife and I visited Ireland and were taking a tour of some monastic ruins. In the cathedral, the tour guide pointed to a narrow slit in the upper wall. She called it a "lepers' squint" because that's where the lepers would view the church service below. Because of their condition, they weren't allowed to partake with the rest of the congregation, instead being relegated to "squint" for a glimpse of God through this narrow opening.

As the tour continued on, I stood there for a few moments thinking about the implications of such an invention. On the one hand, it made perfect sense to keep the communicably sick from the general population. On the other, it seemed to reinforce the very separation Jesus came to abolish with His ministry. I couldn't help but think that we've created "squints" in our churches, even though literal lepers are rare. For the last half-century, churches have been moving out of the difficult neighborhoods rather than into them. We've created expectations of those who would attend our churches that they believe, say, and do the "right" things. How many times has someone been looked down upon because we thought they didn't dress appropriately, or hadn't bathed, or simply because their kids didn't know how to behave in a worship service? The "squint" in our churches is often the front door!

Matthew 8:1-4 grabs me every time I read it. It's not a very long story; it's really just a vignette, but it carries a lot of meaning, and speaks volumes about Jesus and His mission in the world. And it speaks volumes about what it means to be an "ugly church" and how being ugly is a good thing.

*When Jesus came down from the mountainside, large crowds followed him. A man with leprosy came and knelt before him and said, "Lord, if you are willing, you can make me clean."*

*Jesus reached out his hand and touched the man. "I am willing," he said. "Be clean!" Immediately he was cleansed of his leprosy. Then Jesus said to him, "See that you don't tell anyone. But go, show yourself to the priest and offer the gift Moses commanded, as a testimony to them."*

Jesus healed a lot of lepers. While the healing part is important, it isn't the definitive point. It's Jesus' interaction with the leper. But first, there are some things you need to know about lepers and leprosy in Jesus' time. First of all, they were considered "unclean," which meant they couldn't be part of society. When Moses gave the Law to Israel, the Law stated that those with certain skin diseases, i.e. lepers, were to be kept outside the camp until they were healed. Then they were allowed back in after an examination by the chief priest and the appropriate sacrifice.

The reason wasn't to punish or banish. It was a way to limit spread of disease in case it was contagious. By Jesus' time, however, lepers weren't simply "kept outside the camp." They were ostracized and cut off from most of society. The common belief was that diseases, particularly incurable ones, were punishment for something they or their parents had done, so there wasn't a terrible amount of sympathy. Leprosy is a wasting disease, so that it was really only a matter of time before a person would likely die from it. Sadly, there were many who would see that as a good thing.

Not only were they kept apart, lepers had to declare their presence by yelling "unclean!" wherever they went. They essentially forfeited their names for this label. This was their identity. It wasn't enough to have a debilitating disease, to be "sick." Their sickness made them "unclean" or unfit for community, for belonging, for simply being human. They were deemed "other" and unwelcome.

To come into contact with an "unclean" person meant becoming unclean yourself. In Moses' time, that person would be kept outside the camp for a period of time, kept out of fellowship with the rest of the people until they were no longer considered "unclean" by the chief priest and made the appropriate sacrifice. So, contact, even coming into close proximity with anything or anyone that was considered unclean, was to be avoided at all cost. You just didn't do it, and certainly not on purpose.

**Love compelled Him to do what no one else would dream of doing, to enter into the ugliness of the leper's life to redeem and restore all that he had lost.**

So, this brings us back to Jesus and the leper. The leper had all the odds stacked against him. If most people didn't want anything to do with him, why would this holy teacher? But the man had faith. He believed that Jesus was capable of healing him. He also had courage, boldly approaching Jesus, despite his condition. Whatever reservation or apprehension he had, it was overcome by his desire to be made "clean."

Remember, being made "clean" wasn't just about being healed of a disease. Being made clean was essentially being made "whole." That which had been taken away—friends, family, community, and even human dignity—would be restored. The separation from others would be removed. The separation from the religious assembly would be removed as well, because as long as the person was unclean, they couldn't visit the temple or attend synagogue. Again, to be made clean was to be made whole.

The leper was asking Jesus to give him his life back. Removing the leprosy was just the beginning. Jesus had every reason to keep His distance, to avoid "contaminating" Himself. But Jesus was more than willing to heal; He was willing to touch the untouchable.

This is what hits me so hard every time. Jesus chose to touch the leper, to bestow humanity, significance, and value on him. Jesus could have called out from a distance, or at least kept His hands to Himself. But He didn't. Love compelled Him to do what no one else would dream of doing, to enter into the ugliness of the leper's life to redeem and restore all that he had lost.

This kind of love is rare, particularly between strangers. The sacrifices we're willing to make for loved ones are admirable compared to the lack of regard so often given for the "lepers" in our midst. Personally, I have done my share of shunning, turning a blind eye and cold shoulder to those God would have me love as myself. Let me share a story.

I grew up in rural Tennessee, in the foothills of the Appalachians, in the late '70s and early '80s. My dad pastored a small country church accessible only by a dirt road that twice forded a creek. For my father's service, he was granted a small parsonage in much need of repair and an even smaller stipend. We lived by the work of our hands on the two or so acres attached to the parsonage, growing vegetables and raising pigs, cows, and chickens. We were poor but not impoverished. More significantly, we were fairly well-off by the living standards around us.

This spectrum of poverty, wherein one can look up the ladder to feel jealousy and down the ladder to feel superior, came into sharp relief through the person of Marvin. Marvin's head was perpetually shaved, partially to save money on haircuts, but more so to deal with the plague of lice that relentlessly stalked his family. His family lived in a shingle-sided farmhouse held upright more from stubbornness than physics. Indoor plumbing, while commonplace in nearly the entire country during this time, was much less so in Appalachia. Marvin's family had a privy in the backyard and a pump for the well. Bathing was a chore and not a convenience, so Marvin came to school smelling of his farm, the animals, and hard work. He was also a bedwetter.

For all my looking up the ladder at other kids who had things better than me, it was Marvin who daily reminded me that I lived a princely life, however poor we were. And it is Marvin who reminds me daily of my failures to love my neighbor as myself. I would like to tell a story about grace and acceptance, how Marvin learned he was loved by God through the kindness of a preacher's kid. But that, sadly, is not how the story goes.

Marvin was among the last kids the school bus picked up every morning. So, by the time he boarded, most seats were taken. If you were lucky enough to have a friend on the route, you would have a full seat, and Marvin would have to find somewhere else to sit. Even though I had little social capital and just a few friends, I feared moving down the ladder by being associated with Marvin. It breaks my heart now to think about treating him like everyone else treated him: avoiding eye contact, leaving as little room in our seats so that he would pass us by, and ignoring him when we did find ourselves sharing a seat with him.

If I bear a thorn in my flesh, it is the raw regret I carry for the Marvins in my life that didn't see Jesus in me, for those whom I didn't deem worthy to receive the kind of belonging and acceptance I so desperately craved for myself. That which I feared I was not worthy of, I withheld from one in even more need.

I can't help but wonder how Jesus would have treated Marvin. He would have greeted him every day, eager to have Marvin sit with him on the bus. He would have even saved him a seat. He would have gotten to know Marvin, not just the undesirable things that made the rest of us keep our distance. Marvin may have been smart and funny, with unknown talents waiting to be shared...or not. Either way, Marvin carried the image of God and we couldn't look past his "ugly" exterior. Just like with the leper, Jesus would have restored Marvin's dignity and value. Who were we to take those from him in the first place?

**Here's the truth: we all have a leper inside us.**

Here's the truth: we all have a leper inside us. Most of us, (all of us?), harbor regrets, guilt, shame, secrets and sins that have convinced us that we are untouchable and that if we were honest about them, we'd be cast out. We would be repulsive to others. Worse, we may question God's love for us. We think, "How could a Holy God love a sinner like me?" We question it, because we struggle to love ourselves. We don't see ourselves as God sees us, and we struggle even more to do the same for others. We've ostracized the leper in ourselves, and have become unwilling to let Jesus and the leper meet. And so, we are not healed. We are

**Somewhere along the line, the Church got pretty. Right behavior got put ahead of belonging and belief, so that only the most qualified were welcome.**

not whole. What we're not willing to do for ourselves we are even less likely to do for others.

When we dare to acknowledge the leper in ourselves, we can shed any false pride toward others. We can accept and embrace that our rotten stuff doesn't stink less than anyone else's. Just as Jesus willingly touched us, we willingly touch the lives of other "untouchables." Truly, there is no such thing as untouchable. We embrace as we have been embraced, love as we have been loved, so that they may know the same Healer that has healed us and granted us full and abundant life.

The beauty of the Church isn't its appearance. It surely isn't because everyone is perfect or that everything is done perfectly. The beauty of the Church is found in the transformation of those declared "ugly"/repulsive by the world into the beautiful creations that God always intended. Somewhere along the line, the Church got pretty. Right behavior got put ahead of belonging and belief, so that only the most qualified were welcome. So much so that those on the outside thought they needed to get fixed before they could get in. Imagine the leper thinking he needed to heal himself before he could meet Jesus. If that was the case, why would he need Jesus? Woe to the gatekeepers and "Kingdom bouncers" who would keep out the "riff-raff"! For where would we be without grace?

The leper reminds us that we can find healing in Jesus Christ and that anyone can find healing, wholeness, and life in Christ. Which means, it seems to me, that the Church ought to be in the business of seeking "lepers" rather than shunning them.

**Woe to the gatekeepers and "Kingdom bouncers" who would keep out the "riff-raff"! For where would we be without grace?**

# Chapter

# 3

# The One Among the Many

We live in a celebrity-driven culture, even within the Church. We're lying to ourselves if we think otherwise. Don't we look up to the big names in Christian culture? The pastors of megachurches, or the leaders of mega- or terra-ministries? Don't we aspire to be more like the trendsetters of the culture? Some part of our middle-school selves remains and is still hung up on fitting in and not being left behind. We look around and hope for the approval of our peers. We forget Whose approval we really need.

When Jesus' disciples argued about who among them was greatest in the Kingdom, Jesus had to reorient their thinking. In truth, He had to turn it upside down. The economics of the Kingdom are antithetical to that of the world: in order to be first, you have to be last. Instead of

**I think the all-stars in heaven will be the ones no one knew about. They will not have books written about them; they won't have done speaking or book tours; they will have just loved and served in the heavenly spotlight of anonymity.**

standing on the backs of others to achieve greatness, you have to allow others to stand on your back. Because of this, I think the all-stars in heaven will be the ones no one knew about. They will not have books written about them; they won't have done speaking or book tours; they will have just loved and served in the heavenly spotlight of anonymity.

Jesus found Himself in the company of the powerful on many occasions. He wasn't fazed by their status or authority in the world. His greatness manifested itself most profoundly in His interactions with the lowliest and least influential like blind beggars and lepers. And Jesus had a habit of telling those He healed to keep quiet about what had happened. Imagine a celebrity of any stripe doing any charitable thing today without having a mob of press to document it and invite showers of accolades.

Not only did Jesus not seek the approval of people, He didn't play favorites. The rich and powerful didn't have any greater access to Him than the poor and powerless. I imagine it was frustrating for those accustomed to getting their own way.

In Mark 5:21-34 we read about Jesus being approached with a desperate need. Jairus, a leader in the local synagogue, comes to Jesus because his daughter is dying and hopes Jesus may save her. Jesus, as one would expect, immediately makes His way to Jairus' house.

The going can't be easy because Jesus is surrounded by a crowd. The more He heals, the more He ministers, the greater His reputation and the larger the crowds. They are pressing in all around Him. In the midst of this mob, Jesus is making His way to Jairus' daughter. And it's in the middle of this crowd that something happens. A woman who had been bleeding for as long as Jairus' daughter had been alive, fights through the crowd with one goal— just to touch the hem of Jesus' garment, just the edge of His cloak. She tells herself that if she can just get that little piece of Jesus, she can have relief. And she's willing to do whatever she has to get that one touch that could change her life.

Mark writes that she has tried doctors of various kinds and impoverished herself in the search for healing. Nothing has worked, only made things worse. Now she has heard about this Jesus, this rabbi, this prophet, this man of God who makes the lame to walk, the blind to see, and the sick to be well. You can only imagine the depth of her desperation as she fights through the crowd. You can only imagine her audacity and courage, for like the leper, she is unclean because of her hemorrhaging; thus, every person she touches as she makes her way to Jesus could be considered unclean as well. If she could just touch the tassel hanging from Jesus' tunic... When she touches Jesus' clothes, power goes out from Jesus and the woman's bleeding stops. The uncontrollable bleeding is controlled, the chaos ceases.

Jesus could have continued on without breaking stride. He's got a dying girl to get to. But Jesus needed to know who, what, and why. Who was this person? What was their story?

So, Jesus stops and asks who touched Him. You can almost hear the sarcasm in the disciples' response. "In case you didn't notice, Jesus, you're in a crowd!" But Jesus kept looking. Despite her fear, she confesses. She knows that she has crossed some lines: she's unclean because of her condition, and yet is in the crowd; moreover, she is trying to touch this Teacher and Healer without permission. But she's desperate, and she confesses that desperation to Jesus.

It's important for this woman to come face to face with Jesus, for Jesus to articulate and confirm what has happened for the woman's sake. She needs to know that it is her faith that has healed her. It wasn't anything special about Jesus' clothes. Her faith made healing possible.

She needs to know that the suffering is over. "Go in peace and be freed from your suffering." This isn't a brief respite. This isn't a placebo. The days of suffering, of being repulsive and ugly to others are over. The stigma and shame are no more. She is addressed as "Daughter," as one who belongs, one who is valued, one who is loved. The woman's need was one among many needs and expectations that pressed in constantly on Jesus. Among all the needs, she still mattered. And in case you've missed the point, you matter!

While all this is happening, Jairus is waiting. And in that waiting, some people from Jairus' house come and say it's too late. The girl has died. Don't bother Jesus anymore. In that moment, how frustrating would it be for Jairus? If only they hadn't delayed. If only they had hurried and gotten away from the crowd. If only this unclean woman--this outcast--hadn't slowed them all down...

But Jesus' mission is undeterred. He needs one thing from Jairus: to stand firm in his faith. This is typical Jesus: rebuking fear and encouraging faith. Jesus takes just His inner circle (Peter, James, and John) and goes into the place where the little girl is lying. Jesus

**Each of us is one among many, but we matter. Each of us is important, valued, and loved.** encourages those in the house, telling them that the girl is only asleep. All He gets in return is mockery. This has been a day of sarcasm and cynicism...but Jesus is undeterred. He commands the girl to rise, and she does so immediately.

Jesus accomplishes both: He heals and resurrects. He is capable and available to the the least and the greatest. How often do we feel like the hemorrhaging woman? How often do we feel like Jesus is too busy with "real" problems that we don't dare come to Jesus boldly? Who are we to bother Him? Are we desperate enough to do whatever it takes to find peace and freedom from suffering? Each of us is one among many, but we matter. Each of us is important, valued, and loved.

I'm encouraged by this! He's not too busy for me. My anxieties, my worries, my struggles matter to Him. Nothing is too great or too small. As ministers of the Gospel, as Jesus' disciples doing His work in the world, we have to remember this. Are we so focused on some great need on the horizon that we fail to see the needs under our noses? For example, I know a church that does a great job of raising money for overseas missions but makes no effort to address those struggling in their own neighborhood. We can't have tunnel vision in following Jesus.

There's a specific detail in this story that is particularly relevant to us, our mission and vision as followers of Christ. It speaks volumes about God's heart, the mission of Jesus, and the upside-down nature of the Kingdom of heaven. Jairus was a person of some importance. He was a leader in the local synagogue, which carried with it some authority and recognition. The woman, on the other hand, wasn't even allowed in the door of the synagogue because of her condition. Jesus makes no distinction between the value of the two. Whatever value system the world has placed on them—one a man, the other a woman, both coming to Jesus in desperation, one in authority, one on the fringes—has no effect on their value in the Kingdom. No one is loved any less. None of us. No one.

It seems most of the lessons I learn, I must learn through failure. Sometimes we have our sights set on doing the "great" things for God, when the truly great things are seemingly very small. In my young adult years, I had rock star dreams. My friends and I had a band and played anywhere we could. At the time, we were part of a house church called Our Father's House. Part of this church included a communal dwelling called Cottage House, named for the street it was on. Cottage House was home to 20 or so artists, transients, men and women in recovery, and nonconformists trying to figure out how to follow Jesus, and doing so in community. The bass player and drummer of my band called Cottage House home, and as part of the church I got to know everyone in the house.

Two of the residents were father and son. The father had been a heroin addict for his entire adult life and the son, Chris, struggled with meth and alcohol. Chris was a talented musician, but lousy student. He had dropped out of high school before becoming part of the community at Cottage House. They were embraced by Our Father's House, and the people in the church came around them to support them any way they could. In the two or so years Chris and his dad were part of the fellowship, they experienced success and failure in their recovery, but mostly success. Then, after selling my ten-speed bike to the dad so he could get to work, the dad disappeared and Chris followed suit soon after. Nothing was heard from them.

We grieved for them, assuming their addictions were to blame for their abrupt disappearances, and prayed for them and wondered if we would see them again. A few years later, Our Father's House disbanded and the residents of Cottage House dispersed. Chris and his dad hadn't returned. I had moved on with life--but still pursuing rock star dreams--and gotten engaged. It was on a lunch date with my fiance--now wife--that Chris's path and mine would cross.

Panhandlers commonly occupy the downtown sidewalks and the key to not giving up your hard-earned cash is to avoid eye contact and appear occupied with something else. Better yet, if you happen to be with someone else, you can pretend you don't see the panhandler or hear their plea for change. Walking with my fiance, I employed the latter strategy as we approached a young man in dirty clothes and

**Like Saul receiving his sight, my eyes cleared and I recognized Chris, gaunt, haggard, and wearing the wounds of methamphetamine use. Suddenly, this stranger was a friend.** matted hair sitting on the sidewalk and leaning against a building. As we got closer, I intentionally spoke a little louder so that it was obvious we were preoccupied. But as we passed by, the young man called my name. "Andrew!" It took a moment to process that the beggar knew my name. "Andrew!" Like Saul receiving his sight, my eyes cleared and I recognized Chris, gaunt, haggard, and wearing the wounds of methamphetamine use. Suddenly, this stranger was a friend. I pushed down the whelming guilt and shame so that I could ask how he was. Homeless, hungry, and harried by his addiction, he was not well.

Still embarrassed from having ignored him, we invited Chris to lunch and treated him to the first real meal he'd had in a while. Even though we wanted to help more, despite not really knowing how, Chris would thank us for lunch and head back out to the street. While that moment may have only meant a full belly for Chris (I never saw him again after that), it convicted me deeply. Even though I had been part of what I would call an example of an "ugly church," I had forgotten what it meant to love the unlovely, to identify with the outsider.

While many of us wouldn't be comfortable with the model of Our Father's House, the loose polity or communal living, it had one thing undeniably correct. People had to know they belonged before they could believe in a God that loved them. Through belonging, they grew to believe, and their hearts and minds were transformed. They were still artists and largely transient, recovering, and nonconforming, and they were adopted into the family of God. Chris, in all his struggles and suffering, never ceased to be a child of God. He never ceased to be one for whom Christ died and one for whom the ninety-nine were left behind.

Whatever I thought I was to do for the Kingdom, it wasn't greater than Chris. It still isn't. There are crowds around us desperate for just a little piece of Jesus, but will we take the time to notice them and love them like Jesus?

# Chapter

# 4

## Letting in the Riff-raff

Tennessee summers are hot and oppressively humid. It's like wearing a wet wool blanket every day. Miserable. So, you can imagine the total heaven of a cool swimming pool when summer gets into full swing.

After we moved off the farm, we moved to a town of about 13,000 people, which felt like a city. It had a Wal-Mart, so it was kind of a big deal. It also had two swimming pools. One was public, and the other was private. The public pool was routinely closed due to health violations, water quality, lack of funding, etc. The local river was the next best bet, unless you had access to the private pool.

The private pool belonged to an athletic club, so you had to be a member or be the guest of a member. My family weren't members, but I had a friend across town whose family was. Needless to say, I invited myself along any time I could to that pristine,

**Privilege, boils down to access. Access to the better things in life: better schools, better neighborhoods, better stores, better healthcare, better opportunities...**

sparkling oasis. It wasn't chaotic and overcrowded like the public pool. Not everyone could get in, so I felt special, at least by association.

Privilege, I think, boils down to access. Access to the better things in life: better schools, better neighborhoods, better stores, better healthcare, better opportunities... Access is exclusive in order to have value. If everyone has the same access, where's the privilege? What then is special about it? The value of a Harvard education, for

**Jesus isn't a commodity, but those around Him treated Him as if He were.** example, is only partially in the quality of the education; much of its value is in the limited access to that education and what access that education allows. Those on the inside necessarily want to keep access limited. The rarer a commodity, the more value it has.

Jesus isn't a commodity, but those around Him treated Him as if He were. There were those around Him, even His disciples, who wanted to be the gatekeepers. They wanted to control access to Jesus.

## The Tax Man

*Mark 2:13-17*

*Once again Jesus went out beside the lake. A large crowd came to him, and he began to teach them. As he walked along, he saw Levi son of Alphaeus sitting at the tax collector's booth. "Follow me," Jesus told him, and Levi got up and followed him.*

*While Jesus was having dinner at Levi's house, many tax collectors and sinners were eating with him and his disciples, for there were many who followed him. When the teachers of the law who were Pharisees saw him eating with the sinners and tax collectors, they asked his disciples: "Why does he eat with tax collectors and sinners?" On hearing this, Jesus said to them, "It is not the healthy who need a doctor, but the sick. I have not come to call the righteous, but sinners."*

One might think that the Son of God would want to hang out with the "righteous" and "important" people. I mean, He came to earth as a baby, endured the ignomity of a human upbringing in a nowhere town in the backwaters of Galilee. And from a strategic standpoint, wouldn't it make sense to target the leaders and teachers, those with authority who could get things done?

Jesus' mission wasn't to those who felt they had already arrived in places of privilege and position. They weren't open to the message of Jesus; they didn't acknowledge the sin and need in their lives.

So Jesus went after the ripe fruit, those that had no illusions about their separation from God. Jesus said, "I have come to call not the righteous but sinners. It is the sick that need a physician, not the healthy."

It's kind of a trick answer to the accusation made by His critics, for no one is righteous. However, the Pharisees and teachers of the Law were certain they were. And they felt that there were to be the gatekeepers. They interpreted the Law; they defined who was righteous or unrighteous, they cast judgment on whomever didn't meet their criteria for holiness.

The Pharisees were about behavior first, and belief second. Only if you acted right and assented to the teaching of the religious leaders could you belong. Jump through the hoops, check the boxes, and then the doors would be open. But Jesus tossed this mentality on its head. When Jesus approached Levi, He didn't do so expecting Levi to get his act together first. And He didn't quiz Levi on his knowledge of the Scriptures. He simply said, "Follow me," and then went and had dinner with Levi and his friends, commonly referred to as "sinners". Jesus said by His actions, "You matter. You are loved." Jesus knew what we tend to overlook—that belief and behavioral change often follow a sense of belonging and relationship. In this case, belonging came first and life change followed. Jesus was granting access when the Pharisees were guarding the door.

## The Blind Beggar

*Mark 10:46-52*

*Then they came to Jericho. As Jesus and his disciples, together with a large crowd, were leaving the city, a blind man, Bartimaeus (which means "son of Timaeus"), was sitting by the roadside begging. When he heard that it was Jesus of Nazareth, he began to shout, "Jesus, Son of David, have mercy on me!"*

*Many rebuked him and told him to be quiet, but he shouted all the more, "Son of David, have mercy on me!"*

*Jesus stopped and said, "Call him."*

*So they called to the blind man, "Cheer up! On your feet!*

*He's calling you." Throwing his cloak aside, he jumped*

*to his feet and came to Jesus.*

*"What do you want me to do for you?" Jesus asked him.*

*The blind man said, "Rabbi, I want to see."*

*"Go," said Jesus, "your faith has healed you." Immedi-*

*ately he received his sight and followed Jesus along the*

*road.*

Blind Bartimaeus is one of my favorite people in the entire Bible, because he is the model of desperation for Jesus. I love Bartimaeus's courage to cry out, and to be undeterred by those around him. I love that he threw off his cloak, the only thing he had of value, to make his way to Jesus. That's the kind of desire I want to have for Jesus every day of my life.

One of the more painful things about this story, for me, is how much I can see myself in the crowd. When Bartimaeus starts making noise, the crowd tells him to shut up. They "rebuke" him, which means they basically tell him that it's not his place to speak up--he's being denied access. It's not his place to make noise or draw attention to himself. He's a blind beggar, of no consequence, so he should shut up and go away. Bart is creating a scene, being disorderly, making things awkward. He's interrupting whatever is going on around Jesus. It's uncomfortable, and no one likes discomfort.

I'm a fan of things being orderly. I'm not a fan of the status quo, but I'm also not a fan of chaos. How would I respond to Bart making a scene as I'm trying to listen to Jesus? Would I tell him to shut up? Would I try to ignore him and hope he goes away? Or would I acknowledge that he needs Jesus and make a way for him to get to Jesus?

The crowd is so fickle. First, they deny access to Jesus, until Jesus corrects them. Then they seem overeager to get Bart to Jesus. They still want to control—or pretend to control—access to Jesus.

## The Little Ones

*Mark 10:13-16*

*People were bringing little children to Jesus for him to*

*place his hands on them, but the disciples rebuked them.*
*When Jesus saw this, he was indignant. He said to them,*
*"Let the little children come to me, and do not hinder*
*them, for the kingdom of God belongs to such as these.*
*Truly I tell you, anyone who will not receive the kingdom*
*of God like a little child will never enter it." And he took*
*the children in his arms, placed his hands on them and*
*blessed them.*

Jesus had soft spots for the least empowered. Among the least empowered were children. It's one thing to have the Pharisees or the crowds attempting to control access to Jesus and the Kingdom, but what about the disciples? What about this group that has been following Jesus and learning from Him, witnessing Him interact with people of every stripe and stratum? Here we find the disciples being the gatekeepers.

It makes some sense that the disciples would be watching out for Jesus. The demands on His time and energy are constant. The needs are endless. The opportunities to demonstrate the Kingdom of heaven are all around, at every turn. So when some parents bring their children to Jesus to be blessed, the disciples feel like they need to guard the door, so to speak. But Jesus takes the **Jesus had soft spots for the least empowered.** opportunity to teach the disciples a much-needed lesson. The Kingdom is open to all who would be like these children, with eyes and hearts wide open, with faith that isn't jaded or contractual. When you put young children together, they figure out how to play together. They make up games and ways to enjoy each other. They develop instant community, express openness to others, and approach others without pre-judgment. They receive truth and love without skepticism.

Those who should have known better, who themselves had been granted access to the Kingdom, wanted to "guard the door." Jesus was always granting access to Himself and thus to the Kingdom. His "love first" way of doing things

**The Kingdom is open to all who would be like these children, with eyes and hearts wide open, with faith that isn't jaded or contractual.**

goes against the grain of religious insiders, then and now. Jesus wanted the least, last, and lost to know first and foremost that they were loved. When they knew they mattered, they were open to believing in Jesus. Did all the people at Levi's party decide to follow Jesus? Probably not. But some surely did. And those who believed were transformed.

**His "love first" way of doing things goes against the grain of religious insiders, then and now.**

We're not called to keep the riff-raff out. We were the riff-raff--and some of us still are! Would-be gatekeepers see it this way: behavior first, belief second, and belonging last. When the Church was the center of social and cultural life, that might have had some weight, even if it was unbiblical. Hang belonging over their head, and that might get them to change their behavior or belief. But especially now in a post-Christian world, belonging has to come first. Belief and behavior will follow. Love first. That's one of the reasons it's called "ugly church."

If the church prioritizes loving people wherever they are, whatever state they're in, whatever condition, wherever they are in their journey of faith, the church will be full of people who don't know how to "behave." It will be full of people who have incomplete or incorrect theology--or no theology at all! It will be full of people whose lives are being changed, and that's a messy business. But that's the "business" of the Church, because this "business" is the mission of Jesus Christ, its Head.

We've talked about Jesus touching the leper in the process of healing him and how Jesus declared through His actions that no one is untouchable. We've looked at the woman who snuck through the crowd to touch Jesus' clothes so that she could be healed of a hemorrhage that had been plaguing her for 12 years. Even though Jesus was

**If the church prioritizes loving people wherever they are, whatever state they're in, whatever condition, wherever they are in their journey of faith, the church will be full of people who don't know how to "behave."**

**The Church isn't meant to be pretty in any way we understand prettiness.** on His way to see the dying daughter of a person of some importance, He took the time to make sure this woman who people saw as unimportant knew that she mattered, was valued and loved.

The Church isn't meant to be pretty in any way we understand prettiness. It's beautiful because of its "ugliness," where the riff-raff have access to Jesus, lepers are embraced, and the dead find new life. None of us have our acts totally together. We're all in some state of repair. Ours is to be an ugly church, where everyone is invited into the Lord's workshop to be made whole and complete. Where everyone has access to Jesus, to the One who laid down His life for us all. Where everyone has a place at the table no matter their background, color of skin, social status, or size of their bank account. Praise God that He's letting in the riff-raff, because He let in someone like me--and you!

# Chapter

# 5

## Terminally Uncool

We've been talking about being an "ugly" church, a church for the least, last, and lost. We've been talking about touching the "untouchable," embracing the excluded, and following in the footsteps of Jesus that those around Him considered "wrong"—hanging out with the wrong people, going to the wrong places, even healing and saving in the wrong way or the wrong time. Even though Jesus gathered crowds around Him, He was always polarizing. He was never the cool kid that everyone liked or wanted to be like; He was rejected as readily as He was embraced.

To follow Jesus means embracing the fact we'll be terminally uncool. Do you remember that phrase? It seems like something from the '80s, but it's been so long I don't remember when I first heard that phrase. Terminally uncool means being hopelessly and forever uncool. It means never being cool, and any attempts at being cool will be hypocritical. It's a terminal diagnosis without hope of improvement.

As "herd" animals, if you will, we don't like being on the "outside," however it's defined. We're wired for relationship and crave acceptance. Especially when we're younger and trying to figure out who we are and how we fit into the world, most of us strive to be "in" rather than "out." In- is an important prefix. It's found in words like included, involved, and integrated.n Given the choice between "included" and "excluded," included sounds so much better!

Jesus, in His words to the disciples, made many promises, and not all of them sound appealing. We like to cling to those that make us feel good, all warm and fuzzy inside. Promises that He will never leave us nor forsake us. Promises to prepare a place for us, to intercede for us, and to welcome us into eternity. But He also promises persecution. He promises ridicule and opposition in this life. And He promises sacrifice—of everything—if we are to follow Him. Put all that together, and, in the eyes of the world, we are terminally uncool.

*John 15:18-25*

*"If the world hates you, keep in mind that it hated me first. If you belonged to the world, it would love you as its own. As it is, you do not belong to the world, but I have chosen you out of the world. That is why the world hates you. Remember what I told you: 'A servant is not greater than his master.' If they persecuted me, they will persecute you also. If they obeyed my teaching, they will obey yours also. They will treat you this way because of my name, for they do not know the one who sent me. If I had not come and spoken to them, they would not be guilty of sin; but now they have no excuse for their sin. Whoever hates me hates my Father as well. If I had not done among them the works no one else did, they would not be*

*guilty of sin. As it is, they have seen, and yet they have hated both me and my Father. But this is to fulfill what is written in their Law: 'They hated me without reason.'*

As the world treated Jesus, so can we expect to be treated when we look like Him. We will repel and attract. We are not better than Jesus, so why do we aim for a comfortable, hassle-free life? Certainly, if we are making waves for the Kingdom of God, we will face opposition. If you have never experienced resistance in your journey with Jesus, you might question just how much you look like Him.

**If you have never experienced resistance in your journey with Jesus, you might question just how much you look like Him.**

*1 Cor. 1:18-25*

*For the message of the cross is foolishness to those who are perishing, but to us who are being saved it is the power of God. For it is written:*

*"I will destroy the wisdom of the wise;*

*the intelligence of the intelligent I will frustrate."*

*Where is the wise person? Where is the teacher of the law? Where is the philosopher of this age? Has not God made foolish the wisdom of the world? For since in the wisdom of God the world through its wisdom did not know him, God was pleased through the foolishness of what was preached to save those who believe. Jews demand signs and Greeks look for wisdom, but we preach Christ crucified: a stumbling block to Jews and foolishness to Gentiles, but to those whom God has called, both Jews and Greeks, Christ the power of God and the wisdom of God. For the foolishness of God is wiser than human wisdom, and the weakness of God is stronger than human strength.*

You get it, or you don't. It is foolishness until it isn't. From the outside looking in, does the Gospel make sense? It's scandalous, this thought that our Savior died on a cross. Unless we recognize our own sinfulness that necessitated Christ's death, His death is meaningless to us. But when you get it, you get it.

It was a week or so before Easter of 1983 and some movie about Jesus' crucifixion was playing on TV. I was nine years old and had spent my entire life in the Church. As I watched Jesus being nailed to the cross, a light went on. All the sermons and Sunday School lessons pointed to this new understanding. In that moment I got it. He was dying for me. And I wept—I bawled! My eyes still sting when I think about it. What was foolishness before became all wisdom. Scandal became salvation.

## Trying too Hard to be Cool

To be fully committed to following Jesus is to be terminally un-cool—sometimes even in the eyes of Christian culture. It seems like the Church largely keeps itself busy with chasing after the cool kids. The mega/terra churches can afford the flash and bang of high production value, and the smaller churches do what they can to keep up. We don't want to be uncool in the eyes of the world or other churches. To choose ugliness is to go in the opposite direction.

The commission of the Church, in short, is to introduce people to Jesus. We bear witness to what God has done in our lives by telling our stories--the good, the bad, and the ugly. Our lives are highlight reels of forgiveness and mercy, of redemption and reconciliation. We show the love of Christ by entering into the muck and mire of messy lives, offering grace over condemnation. We proclaim the Good News and don't care if we look foolish in the process.

When the messy and broken gather, things get awkward. There's little polish or panache, just real people getting real with one another, beating their chests and crying out for mercy. The ugly church isn't just open to awkwardness; it perseveres through it and sees God at work in it. Pretend and pretense fall away in the light of God's amazing grace.

Jesus' ministry was awkward. He collected the rabble and the rejects wherever He went. The "unclean" waded through the "clean" to get to Him. Four friends perpetrated a "B and E" (breaking and entering) on someone's house to get their friend in front of Jesus to be healed. Blind beggars and lepers sought Him out, even if they made others uncomfortable.

A church that looks like Jesus' awkward and ugly ministry isn't going to be very attractive or "cool." And it probably isn't going to be very "successful" by the standards of the world that have been adopted by the Church.

Buildings, budgets, and butts—this is what the Church has borrowed from the world. Bigger, better buildings, bigger budgets, and bountiful butts in the seats. This is what we have come to believe to be success. By these measures, many of us would consider ourselves to be failures. And many of us have been failing for a long time. And we've been beating ourselves up about it for a long time. Don't we look at the church down the street or across town with the nice building, the great programs, the professional music, etc. and say to ourselves, "That's a successful church"? I pray to God that they are. The exterior stuff that makes others jealous isn't what God judges as successful. But it's the first thing we look at.

If the mission of the church is to point people to Jesus, the question we have to ask ourselves is simply this: are we pointing to Jesus with every bit of our time, talent, and treasure? Are we inviting the wayward and wandering to meet Jesus as enthusiastically as we are to check out our great programs and services? And if we don't feel like we have top-notch programs and services, does that hinder us from inviting them to our churches? Is our "uncoolness" hindering the gospel because we're embarrassed to be seen as awkward and uncool? Is it more embarrassing than when we have to explain to Jesus face to face that we were ashamed of Him?

We have to use God's measure of what it means to be successful: Take a minute to read Matthew 25:14-30.

We tend to look at this parable as a lesson on fruitfulness. The one who receives 5 bags of gold manages to double the master's money, the one with two does the same. But the one who receives one bag of gold buries it in the ground. The two that did something with their bags of gold are rewarded. The one that did nothing is punished.

What we don't pay enough attention to is the master's response. What is he rewarding? Is it the increase on their investment? Through a purely monetary/capitalist lens, we might think so. It's not the increase, it's their faithfulness that the master acknowledges. He says, "Well done, good and faithful servant." They did something with what they were given. They recognized the value of what they were entrusted with and were faithful in their use of it.

In contrast, the servant with the single bag operated out of fear. He feared risking what he was given, scared that he might lose rather than gain. And maybe he didn't place a lot of value in that bag of gold, looking at his fellow servants and their multiple bags with jealousy. We don't realize that we are God's treasure, and whether God has entrusted us with many resources or very few,

**Ugly churches, those that intentionally and purposefully seek the least, last, and lost, underfunded and unpolished, sincere and often small, aren't the "cool" kids. And it's okay.** it's about being faithful with what we're given.

Ugly churches, those that intentionally and purposefully seek the least, last, and lost, underfunded and unpolished, sincere and often small, aren't the "cool" kids. And it's okay. Cool doesn't work among the uncool. Jesus said that He came to call those who know they're sick, not the ones who think they're healthy. The churches on the fringe, in the trenches, are most often the churches of the bruised, broken, and bleeding, but are also places of healing. This is who we are called to be.

The more we look like Jesus, the less "cool" we're going to be. The more we look like Jesus, the more "attractive" we will be to those the world calls "unattractive," not because of ourselves, but because of Christ IN us.

Paul writes to the church in Corinth about the division between those that claimed to be followers of Apollos and those of Paul. Paul made it clear that he and Apollos were just gardeners, planting seeds, watering, and tending to the field. God provides the harvest. They were to be faithful followers of Christ, and God would bring about the growth. And so it is with us: we are to be faithful in the field He has placed us. And we may never be the cool kids, even in the eyes of the Church, but that's not who we're working for. May we be faithful to the mission Christ has given all believers, so that when we are at the end of our time here on earth, we will be welcomed into eternity by the words: "well done, good and faithful servant."

# Chapter

# 6

# A Scandalous Savior

*Isaiah 53:1-3*

*Who has believed our message and to whom has the arm of the Lord been revealed?* **He grew up before him like a tender shoot, and like a root out of dry ground. He had no beauty or majesty to attract us to him, nothing in his appearance that we should desire him. He was despised and rejected by mankind, a man of suffering, and familiar with pain. Like one from whom people hide their faces he was despised, and we held him in low esteem.** *(emphasis added)*

Think about Isaiah's words for a moment. Is there anything in his description of the Messiah that is very attractive? With a description like this, is it any wonder that most people looked past Him for a supermodel/pro athlete/wealthy/worldly type of messiah? Would we recognize Jesus if we came face to face with Him in our churches, at the supermarket, or on the street? We may not because that's not our idea of what a hero looks like.

When looking for a hero, the inclination is to look to the halls of power, to places both important and impressive. It would make sense to look to the palaces and cathedrals, the grand and glorious. That's where you would expect a hero to be. You wouldn't typically look to the alleys and soup kitchens. You wouldn't tend to look to the places where the broken go, the bars and basements, the edges and fringes.

As we've already seen, Jesus hangs out with the wrong crowd, on purpose. He willingly associates with the rough and ragged. He routinely

**You wouldn't tend to look to the places where the broken go, the bars and basements, the edges and fringes.**

does "wrong" things like healing on the sabbath. Like touching lepers. He doesn't seek recognition or glory for Himself. At the height of His popularity, He rides into Jerusalem on a donkey instead of a warhorse. He's constantly turning the understanding of who the Messiah is on its head. He proclaims an upside down kingdom that restructures the world's pecking order. He flips over tables and the status quo. He embodies the messiah described by Isaiah but people weren't looking for a suffering servant; they were looking for an earthly hero.

The apostle Paul describes Jesus in this way:

*Philippians 2:5-8*

*In your relationships with one another, have the same mind-set as Christ Jesus:*
*Who, being in very nature God,*
*did not consider equality with God something to be used to his own advantage;*
*rather, he made himself nothing*

*by taking the very nature of a servant,*

*being made in human likeness.*

*And being found in appearance as a man,*

*he humbled himself*

*by becoming obedient to death—*

*even death on a cross!*

**Jesus even saves the "wrong" way. Instead of making all things right, right now, He steps into the imperfect now, leading us into the perfect to come.**

Jesus even saves the "wrong" way. Instead of making all things right, right now, He steps into the imperfect now, leading us into the perfect to come. Instead of merely addressing the symptoms, He came to fix the underlying problem of separation from God, and all the ramifications of that separation.

Jesus dies the wrong way. It isn't heroic. He doesn't die in battle, and isn't given a noble death. For example, a Roman citizen in Jesus' time would be beheaded, quick and relatively painless and private. An official, or someone else important, might be allowed to drink poison.

Jesus is killed as the lowest of the low. He's hung on a rugged wooden cross—the most humiliating, slow, and painful method of Roman execution—between two common thieves. He's put on display, mocked, and murdered.

Jesus' death is scandalous because in the eyes of the world, a crucified savior isn't much of a savior. For those watching Jesus die, is it unreasonable for them to wonder about His ability to save if He won't save Himself? And what kind of savior dies such a humiliating death, who doesn't overpower and overcome those who beat Him, spat on Him, and nailed Him to the cross?

What is mind-blowing and seemingly foolish is that the message preached by the apostles hinges on Jesus Christ and His crucifixion! It's not an unfortunate detail or a side-note. It is at the center, for they recognize that without His death, there is no salvation. Without Jesus' sacrifice, sin—and death—win. The lowly nature of His death means that no one can say, "He died for better people than me." Even in His death, Jesus identifies with the lowest of the low, the least of the least.

Again and again Paul describes his message as "preaching Christ

**The lowly nature of His death means that no one can say, "He died for better people than me." Even in His death, Jesus identifies with the lowest of the low, the least of the least.**

and Christ crucified." As Christians, we wear the scandal as a badge of honor. Unlike those who mocked Jesus as He hung on the cross, we know the rest of the story. We know that the grave could not contain Him. We know that sin and death were defeated in His death and resurrection. We know that there is hope and life for all who believe.

Our Savior is a scandalous savior. He doesn't fit molds or expectations. Scripture tells us that He wasn't particularly attractive. He came from the wrong town, Nazareth. He had an inauspicious birth, born in a barn. His mom got pregnant before marrying Joseph—so you can imagine the gossip around that! He hangs around the wrong people, does the wrong things, saves humanity the wrong way, and even dies the wrong way. He defies convention and expectation.

The "ugly" church doesn't invite people to rally around a superhero, as we understand a superhero to be—attractive, musclebound, and the center of attention. Our Savior set aside the riches of glory to take on the limits and lowliness of humanity, to live as we live, for the express purpose of laying down that life for the whole of humanity.

I don't know if you ever notice these, but in pop culture and all around us, there are what I call "Christ moments". They weren't intended to be an analogy or a picture of Christ, but they're there if you look.

**Our Savior set aside the riches of glory to take on the limits and lowliness of humanity, to live as we live, for the express purpose of laying down that life for the whole of humanity.**

In the first Captain America movie, Steve Rogers, who becomes Captain America, is introduced as this little guy, short and scrawny. He stands up to bullies, even if that means he takes a beating. World War II is raging, he tries to enlist, but repeatedly gets passed over. How can this scrawny guy with poor health possibly help win a war? He finally gets accepted into a special unit and he is surrounded by soldiers one would expect to be a hero, who are bigger, stronger, faster. It's when a grenade is tossed into the middle of the group that each person's character is exposed. Steve, the smallest, weakest, and unlikeliest, jumps on the grenade to save the rest of the group while the would-be heroes run away. It turns out the grenade is a dummy, but in that moment of self-sacrifice, before Steve is transformed into the hero known as Captain America, we see the Christ moment, the willingness to lay down one's life for his comrades. In that moment of the film, I'm reminded of the poor carpenter's son from the nowhere town of Nazareth, choosing to die so that we may live.

Our very spirits cry out for a Savior. So much so that we weave salvation stories into our culture, into the fabric of our shared humanity. Those stories are often twisted, or only contain a glimpse of the truth, but the need for a savior is there. We feel it in our bones, the groaning of a broken world crying out to God for restoration and redemption. And God sent the Savior the world needs, even if He isn't the one the world wants. Even now, the world looks to other saviors, other messiahs, but there is only one Christ, one salvation, one Lamb of God who takes away the sins of the world: our scandalous Lord and Savior, Jesus Christ.

# Chapter

# 7

# Not Just a Pet Project

Obedience is not optional. Jesus told His disciples, "If you love me, you will keep my commands." We've somehow taken that to mean, "Feel free to pick and choose which ones you want to obey." So, we skip the hard stuff and focus only on the easy, while patting ourselves on the back for a job well done.

Does this sound harsh? If this assessment offends you, perhaps it applies to you. It certainly does to me. While I might get a B+ or even an A- in one area, I'm pulling a solid D- in another. I might

**I might be killing it in Personal Piety 101, but totally blowing it in my Sacrificial Service Lab. And I don't think I'm alone.**

be killing it in Personal Piety 101, but totally blowing it in my Sacrificial Service Lab. And I don't think I'm alone.

In the Church, we act as if Jesus called us out of sin and darkness to give us a new and improved set of rules and regulations for living. As if He only wanted to give us a checklist to follow, a new moral code to replace the old one. As a young Christian, I certainly thought that

**Our consumer-driven church culture has trained Jesus-followers to be spectators rather than participants in the mission of Christ and His kingdom.**

much of following Jesus was simply avoiding bad things, bad words, bad situations, and bad people. But is this what Jesus meant when He said, "Follow me"?

For many Christians, following Jesus looks like this: go to church, sing some songs, hear a sermon, give a little money, shake some hands, and then go home. Maybe during the week hit up a Bible study. Praying and reading the Bible gets squeezed in there if there's time. Our consumer-driven church culture has trained Jesus-followers to be spectators rather than participants in the mission of Christ and His kingdom.

Jesus laid out His mission and as His Church, we have been commissioned and entrusted with that mission.

Luke 4:14-21

*Jesus returned to Galilee in the power of the Spirit, and news about him spread through the whole countryside. He was teaching in their synagogues, and everyone praised him.*

*He went to Nazareth, where he had been brought up, and on the Sabbath day he went into the synagogue, as was his custom. He stood up to read, and the scroll of the prophet Isaiah was handed to him. Unrolling it, he found the place where it is written:*

*"The Spirit of the Lord is on me,*

*because he has anointed me*

*to proclaim good news to the poor.*

*He has sent me to proclaim freedom for the prisoners*

*and recovery of sight for the blind,*

*to set the oppressed free,*

*to proclaim the year of the Lord's favor."*

*Then he rolled up the scroll, gave it back to the atten-*

*dant and sat down. The eyes of everyone in the syn-*

*agogue were fastened on him. He began by saying*

*to them, "Today this scripture is fulfilled in your*

*hearing."*

Jesus read the passage from Isaiah that speaks directly of Him. This is His mission. This is the work that He is sent into the world to do. His target demographic: the poor, imprisoned, blind, and oppressed. The sick and tired, wounded and weary know they need a physician, and Jesus' mission places them squarely in His sights.

It's interesting how we tend to reduce the mission to metaphor. We spiritualize the poor, captive, blind, and oppressed and make it about ourselves to the point that it becomes okay to ignore the literal poor, imprisoned, blind, and oppressed. The good news Jesus proclaims is holistic. Again and again Jesus addressed the physical and spiritual needs of people. He coupled healing with forgiveness; wholeness with reconciliation.

I have the unique privilege of working (and ministering) among those who are often one step from the street or one step from the grave. So, when I hear the words of Jesus, I see the faces of the poor, blind, captive, and oppressed. They have names and individual stories. There is no room for metaphor in their lives; impoverished, blind, captive, and oppressed is

**So, when I hear the words of Jesus, I see the faces of the poor, blind, captive, and oppressed. They have names and individual stories. There is no room for metaphor in their lives; impoverished, blind, captive, and oppressed is simply what they are.**

simply what they are. Engaging these needs creates opportunity to engage their spiritual poverty, blindness, captivity, and oppression.

There are different kinds of poverty: the poor in resources in need of food, clothing, and shelter. The poor in spirit desperate for God and His grace. The poor in community, alone, lonely, and isolated. The poor in purpose, aimless and wandering without direction.

Captivity comes in many forms. Those taken captive by addiction. Those taken captive by an American dream that promises prosperity but too often delivers only more debt and dependence on working harder and longer to achieve that which moth and rust will destroy. Those taken captive by entertainments that distract and draw away from the things of God. Those taken captive by ideologies that warp or take precedence over the mission and message of Christ. False gospels offering cheap grace or promises of prosperity. Political loyalties that outweigh Kingdom ones. Ideologies that foment fear over compassion.

Blindness is a common affliction. Even our own vision is clouded by the lenses of our culture: racism, classism, sexism, nationalism, and various other -isms. We have distorted views of ourselves, of others, of the world, and even of God. If Jesus cautions His disciples to mind the plank in their own eye first, we shouldn't get too busy pointing out the blindness of others until we've dealt with our own. Jesus called out the Pharisees for being "blind guides," which should be cautionary for the Church. Jesus addresses internal, external, physical, and spiritual oppression. In the Church, we tend to focus solely on the spiritual. This was front and center in His ministry as He cast out demons nearly everywhere He went. But not all oppression is spiritual. Many suffer internal oppression from mental illness, anxiety, or depression, or external oppression from violence, instability, or trauma. Many suffer from systems and structures that create or perpetuate injustice and inequality. Jesus had something to say about these things as well.

Perhaps the most beautiful part of the Isaiah passage Jesus reads is the reference to the Year of Jubilee in Leviticus 25. Every Jew in the Nazareth synagogue knew this reference to "the year of the Lord's favor." Every fiftieth year was to be a Jubilee year, when debts were canceled, land returned to its original owners, and slaves set free. It's a reset button for life. No matter how off the rails life gets, no matter how great the debts, no matter the burdens accrued over the previous 49 years, the Year of Jubilee resets it all. This is the essence of salvation, the slate wiped clean, the penalty of sin removed by grace through Jesus Christ.

We recognize in ourselves our need for a Savior that will free us from the bondage of sin, death, darkness, and despair. We're all acquainted with some variation of these: poverty of resources, of spirit, of community, of purpose; blindness to God's love, to the value and needs of others, to reality through God's eyes; captivity to dreams and desires that take precedence over the things of God, to entertainment and distractions, to habits and hurts that rule over us; oppression from without and within, demands of life and others, oppression we feel physically, mentally, emotionally, and spiritually.

Do you feel both the weight and the hope in Jesus' words as He proclaims good news and freedom? When I read these words, my heart swells because I desire them for the people whose faces I see every day and whose names I could list like a litany of misery.

**Good news, freedom, sight, release, the Lord's favor... who of us doesn't desire these things? And if we desire such things for ourselves, how can we withhold them from anyone else?**

Good news, freedom, sight, release, the Lord's favor...who of us doesn't desire these things? And if we desire such things for ourselves, how can we withhold them from anyone else? Jesus' mission is our mission. I wonder when we'll really understand and embrace this truth. It isn't just the mission of the pastor. It isn't just the mission of the missionary or evangelist. It isn't just the mission of the church board members, or the folks on the social action committee. It isn't just the mission of the paid professionals or the radically committed. It's the mission of all of us if we claim to be followers of Jesus Christ.

**When are we going to stop treating our churches like clubs for their members and start seeing them as mission outposts for the kingdom of God?**

So, when is the Church going to stop treating the mission of Jesus like a pet project? When are we going to stop treating our churches like clubs for their members and start seeing them as mission outposts for the kingdom of God? What will it take to be moved out of our comfort and complacency into compassion and self-sacrifice?

Every church has the potential to be an ugly church. If we just look at the others sitting around us on a Sunday morning, there is plenty of ugly to be discovered. We're told to confess our sins to one another so that we can be healed. But how often does confession happen? How often are we willing to get real and raw with our brothers and sisters? If we're not willing to own up to our own messes and step lovingly and graciously into the lives of people we know, how are we ever going to engage and embrace the ugly lives of strangers beyond the walls of our churches?

It is said that proximity breeds familiarity. When names, faces, and individual stories replace stereotypes, relationships can be formed. And in the context of relationship, barriers collapse, bridges are built, and authentic love and friendship takes root. When Mike becomes more than an "addict", Jose more than an "illegal", and Ivan more than a "crazy person", we can begin to see them like Jesus does. I have a hard time picturing Jesus requiring a urine test, documentation, or mental health assessment before allowing access to Himself. We're not familiar with the Mikes, Joses, and Ivans around us because we're too busy guarding the door lest one of them stumbles into our church.

The lepers and the lame, the sick and the searching, the blind and the bound, the ugly and unlovable are in our midst and we're probably somewhere on that list. We're so busy keeping watch that we haven't noticed our own ugliness. We're experts at pretending it doesn't exist. Maybe we just need to remember where we've come from or recognize how far we have yet to go. Amazing things can happen when we're willing to get real with ourselves.

Years ago, I was part of a new church on the growing edge of town, which rocketed from a few dozen to a few hundred in just a couple of years. The congregation first started meeting in a converted machine shop, then built a new sanctuary with a coffee shop and offices to connect the old building to the new. The music and messages moved those that attended; it was a place that encouraged inviting and including others to come check it out.

I served on one of the three worship teams and volunteered with the youth program. The atmosphere energized me to be involved and I looked forward to spending time in ministry. I aspired to be like those I worked alongside because they seemed to have figured out this whole Jesus thing. They exemplified, to me, what a disciple of Jesus looked like. And I didn't think I looked anything like them, at least on the inside.

**I constantly worried that the bloated-whale-carcass-rotting-on-a-beach stench of my real self would be sniffed out.**

Without deliberately trying, the church had gotten pretty. Even though I knew the horrible backstories of those I served with, their present lives seemed to me to be without blemish. I constantly worried that the bloated-whale-carcass-rotting-on-a-beach stench of my real self would be sniffed out. I'd be asked to put down my guitar and leave the premises until the stink was completely and forever gone. This was my fear. Maybe I was too ugly to belong.

Thankfully, I wasn't found out. Instead, something beautiful and liberating happened at our annual men's retreat. I had gotten through most of the retreat without any real danger of being exposed. Maybe I would make it through! On the last night, one of the pillars of the church, a member of the board, stood up in the middle of 100 or so men and confessed to a host of sexual sins: pornography, visiting strip clubs, and even soliciting prostitutes while on business trips. Here was a married man and father, a leader in the church, and someone most of us had looked up to. And here he was laying it all out for the lot of us. And that's when things got ugly.

Man after man stood up and acknowledged their own battles with pornography, among other things. It turned out that the statistics were right--just about every man, including myself, confessed to struggling with online pornography. We had all been carrying around rotting whale carcasses and pretending that the reek didn't belong to us. We thought we had been lying to each other, but we had been lying to ourselves that we were the only ones. With brutal honesty, we got ugly with each other, and I don't know if I've ever witnessed anything so beautiful. I don't exaggerate when I say it changed my life.

And it changed the church. Our conversations were different and deeper. Accountability replaced anonymity, and freedom replaced fear. On that evening of confession, the other guitarist on the worship team and I discovered a common struggle and would walk out of the darkness of our sin together. It's a beautiful memory only made possible by getting ugly.

**If we learn to get ugly with ourselves and with each other, we can get ugly with whomever God brings our way.**

If we learn to get ugly with ourselves and with each other, we can get ugly with whomever God brings our way. A few years after that men's retreat, I was an associate pastor at a different church, overseeing a recovery program that attracted as many as thirty or so on Friday evenings. About a dozen of them would also come to worship service on Sunday morning. And they had no idea how to "behave" in church. They clapped after every song like it was a concert, answered rhetorical questions from the pulpit, and got up for coffee at random times in the service. They came dressed in whatever clothes they had, in whatever shape their clothes were in. And it made the "regular folks" in the church very uncomfortable. Here were people who truly understood how much honesty and authenticity were related to saving their lives, and they didn't know they weren't supposed to be their true selves. It was great because it forced the congregation to put away their plastic masks and get real. If our churches are going to get ugly, we have to start by being brutally honest with ourselves and each other.

It's that kind of honesty, authenticity, and vulnerability that attracts the "unattractive." Broken people feel safest around other broken people.  If they see the broken being made whole, they know there is hope for them, too.  But it requires us to put off the illusion of being "pretty."

We reach out to the poor because we know what it's like to be desperate; we reach out to the captives because we know what it's like to be trapped; we reach out to the blind because we know what it's like to be in darkness; we reach out to the oppressed because we know what it's like to be crushed.  We seek out them out because it's the mission of the One who was pierced for our transgressions and crushed for our iniquities, who took up our pain and bore our suffering, and by whose wounds we are healed.

The mission of Jesus isn't a pet project.  It's the mission of the

Church, universal and entire. It's the mission of terra-, mega-, mini-, micro-, and nano-churches. It's the mission of urban, suburban, and exurban churches. It's the mission of the most remote and rural churches. And it's the mission of every believer in every one of those churches. It's an ugly (and profoundly beautiful) mission that requires an ugly Church made profoundly beautiful by its ugliness. Maybe when we get truly "ugly" the Church will reflect the beauty of Christ.

# Epilogue:

# What now?

The Holy Spirit is at work all around us and it's up to us to be open to His leading and direction. Pray for the Holy Spirit to light a fire in you and your church for ugly ministry. Fervently seek after God's heart, to feel compassion and to grieve over the impoverished, imprisoned, blind, and oppressed. Unless your heart is transformed from stone to flesh, you will never develop a passion for Jesus' mission.

This book was written for the purpose of motivating and mobilizing the Church. A community is growing around this idea of getting ugly for Jesus, and we hope you will get connected as well. The desire is to create a network of support, encouragement, resources, and fellowship among those interested in or already involved in ugly ministry. How you can connect with us:

- Our website: uglychurch.org
- Author's email: andrew@uglychurch.org
- find us on Facebook at @uglychurch and Instagram at ugly. church

Maybe you have been feeling a tug in the direction of ugly ministry. Maybe you've witnessed someone falling through the cracks, or maybe that person was you. If you are looking to get ugly, here are some practical ideas and resources to do that:

- Volunteer at an established ugly ministry or church. Chances are there is a Salvation Army, church-run food bank or clothes closet, homeless shelter, recovery program, prison ministry, elderly outreach, or something similar in your area. Find out how you can help and get your hands dirty.

- Get ugly at your own church.
    o Talk to your pastor or parishioners to find out what needs

aren't being met. Prayerfully construct a strategy and a team to meet those needs, with the expectation of entering into authentic relationship with those in need.

o Create spaces for confession and accountability to deal with the leper inside each of us. Living authentically before God and one another prepares us to live authentically before the world. A real and raw community of Jesus-followers attracts real and raw people in need of Jesus.

o Prayerfully read Ugly Church in your small group or class. Challenge each other to step out of any comfort or complacency that has been holding you back. Ask the Holy Spirit for the wisdom, direction, and boldness you need to go where He leads.

Pray. Share. Connect. Go. It's time to get ugly.

# Acknowledgments

There are several acknowledgments that need to be made, because without the encouragement and assistance of several people, churches, and organizations, this book would not have been written. It would have remained a sermon series reserved for the small gathering of people present to hear it. However, it caught a spark and has grown into a project that we hope God will use to do great things.

First, I have to thank my encouragers, those who spurred me to write, edit, and rewrite, even though I never felt I had the luxury of time to do so. Elisha Cho, friend and fellow pastor, took on the mantle of CEO (Chief Encouragement Officer) and has fulfilled that role faithfully and graciously. His kind words—even when I doubted them—helped me believe that this book was important and worth writing. Day Marshall, my beautiful and brilliant wife of 23 years, whose opinion is never anything but honest, provided objectivity and the necessary space so that this book could get written. She is my both my greatest muse and most valued critic. Without her, this book would never have seen the light of day.

Second, I want to thank the examples that provide inspiration to do the difficult work of loving the "unlovely." Mark Knowlton, who left a comfortable job at a non-profit to launch prison ministries throughout New England for Prison Fellowship. Kurt Gerrold and The Anchor of Hull, Massachusetts, getting deep into the messy lives of individuals and families suffering from addiction and all its consequences. David and Alicia Blais who sold their restaurant to fully invest in Daniel's Table, ending hunger one city at a time. Chuck Pendleton and Eddy Frost, dear friends and colleagues, who exemplify exceptional humility and compassion in ministering to the broken. The list goes on and on. I am deeply moved and inspired by their faithfulness to the mission of Jesus.

The most important example was also the earliest. I'm grateful to Rodney and Kathleen Marshall, and the example of ugly ministry they set for my brother and me from an early age. Our house was routinely filled with strays and castaways, orphans and misfits. We never had so little that there wasn't something to give. There was always room at the table for one more. And there still is.

Next, I want to thank the risk-takers. When I came to the Nazarene

Church in Framingham, Massachusetts, I had never been the lead pastor anywhere. My experience was varied but senior leadership in a local church was lacking. Over the past eight years, the church has graciously been a guinea pig for getting ugly. Community of Grace continues to be an experiment in ugliness, and I'm grateful for their confidence in me and the vision of Ugly Church.

The greatest risk regarding this book was undertaken by the financial backers who, without having read a single word, committed to seeing the first 500 copies published. Ms. Kyo Hee Im of Sido Methodist Church in South Korea, pastor and published author, provided the funding and connections to make this book possible. I am humbled and privileged to be the recipient of such trust.

Lastly, my deepest gratitude belongs forever to Jesus, who continues to invite me along on His mission, despite the great liabilities I bring with me. I'm grateful for His grace as I grow, His love as I learn, and His faithfulness when I fail. I'm never absolutely sure where we're going, but I'm never disappointed when we get there.

*memo*

*memo*

*memo*

*memo*